Crying boys

Crying boys

- April, 2019

Crying boys

CRYING BOYS

Crying boys

Chapter One
Life support　　　…………005

Chapter Two
Dark Imagination　　…………060

Chapter Three
Patience　　　　…………114

Chapter Four
Crying boys　　　…………158

Crying boys

Chapter One

Life support

Crying boys

genesis

my world is like
the beginning of earth
risen from darkness,
the most powerful birth
then there was light,
and then creation
all from the womb
of effortless imagination
from deep seas and the skies,
to people and lands
I intent on having the world in my hands

Crying boys

washing away

my soul and heart
I poured it out
these liquids proceeded down another route
turning tears into bloody trails
calling nights whenever sun rays fail
questioning me about who I love
what are my limits?
where do I stop?
but only tears again
can wash away the blood,
so I must pour it out until it floods

Crying boys

watch me grow

you are the wishes at my feet
moving gradually
spiraling between the grass blades
soaked in the soil under my feet
kissing every worm that crawls
in the dirt of the earth
but this dirt is so beautiful
creating life when it's left to grow alone
cultivating the bloom that we know
I am part of it
now watch me grow

Crying boys

helping hand

the glue that holds my mind together
even when I lose my mind
is my angelic savior,
see they weren't that hard to find
the one loving me like no other
worth all credit of this space
One of a kind, why do I even bother?
nothing that could ever take their place
the one that loves me like no other
affection inside is now all I can see
nobody bothered to tell me
that all along,
this person has always been me

Crying boys

bridge of incidents

tears of happiness
the glimpse of success
faith and confidence is put to the test
was change worth it?
and is it really complete?
have you become the person your life needs?
I hope you are honest
about how you ended up where you are
this is your bridge of incidents,
which means your destination is not that far
this is the bridge you walk
before earning to get what you want

Crying boys

all she demands

my mind is always making love
with some lover loving my mind
undressing the worries off her body
to make love to her all night
her beliefs are my limits
and through her I stay alive
her lovers naked bodies, are all on top me
my feelings are my sacrifice
she gets to make me love,
make me angry, and make me cry
her lovers and I give in to all she demands
but to her, the rules don't apply
she is not dirty from a little sweat,
pillow talk, or a little pain
she is persistent with ever lover she creates
because she knows that every love
has to be maintained
we never get to be things, we always already are
she decides when that will be
and she decides when she breaks our hearts

Crying boys

a music piece of the heart and mind

note after note, you are playing my part
you touch my language, you can feel my art
our music syncs together
our tunes play a song
we are ones and twos, lows and highs
and I will forever sing along
I feel for you, and you speak for me
my instrument is your favorite sound
we match each other perfectly
together, we create a melody

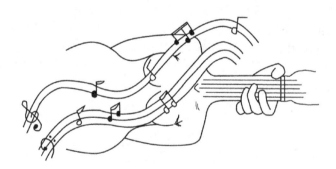

Crying boys

it's all about balance

we are always creating,
and sometimes that's the problem
because creation
does not discriminate,
not against your wildest dreams
nor against disasters

Crying boys

higher you and your lower mind

you are the rage in my paintings
the answer to my questions
the art of seduction
the art of gratitude and patience
you are the admiring raw truth
that everyone wants
but just a few can handle,
and the most resplendent thing
is that you're not and will never
appear in human form
because you always live
somewhere in our minds

Crying boys

tourmaline

I am the tourmaline in ones life
protecting and attacking
the darkness but the light
projecting and reflecting
I'm not on a certain side
I am neither black, nor white
but one thing is for sure
I don't give up without a fight

Crying boys

expectations

perhaps, expectations don't have to exist
if we observe emotions
and take control of our lives
neither should there have to be disappointments
but every expectation has two sides
all might go wrong, all might go right
maybe those were truths, maybe those were lies,
maybe you were right,
but it might have been your pride
in order to make things flow,
we have to put our expectations aside

Crying boys

deciding my story

I always wanted to tell the future
and so I tried
a lot of precognitions telling me stories
until I sometimes wish they lied
but there were also beautiful ones
like love and like birth
who would ever think that my
future wouldn't consist of hurt?
the future looks promising
no delays and no stops
my future knows prosperity
abundance and the card two of cups
I always hated the saying
that better days are to come
because so are bad ones
that's where I gained life experience from
but the high times outdo the low ones
and I'm not bothered by road bumps

Crying boys

the theory is gifted, the practical ,we gift ourselves

I may sound like I got it all figured out
and I sometimes believe
that maybe I do
but knowing all won't give you all
that is the part we have to do our own

Crying boys

make a wish

you are what you want,
and you want what you are
on this journey called life,
no destination can be too far

Crying boys

rabbit hole

I wish,
I wish not much
but when I do,
it involves a touch
a touch of life,
a touch of souls
my feelings fell down
a rabbit hole
I wish not much
but feel those feelings much
until it all weighs down
into my guts
and then I hold on
then I shine
and all I wish
is becoming mine

Crying boys

love yourself

I promise
I won't ever tell you
that you can't be loved
because you don't love yourself
I won't ever tell you
that you are not enough
because you are short on yourself
all I will tell you is
no feeling that you will experience
will compare to self love
and being enough for yourself
so whether you feel it or not
you will be deserving
of whatever you want

Crying boys

roots of our flowers

days went by for
I don't know how long
and the hardest lesson
I then learned
was to let go of the outcome
because holding a flower
too tightly
will destroy it
it will die that way
and it won't flourish
and flourishing
is what I ~~needed~~ need
from you and me

Crying boys

fake it until you make it

you're not sad
there is just too much
for you to comprehend
you will be just fine
until that time
you will have to pretend

Crying boys

misunderstood

conversations can solve problems
the size of national borders
understanding is not that hard
and listening is already half of solving
maybe I don't want to be understood
I find art in causing confusion
simplicity gets boring
and being boring is simply not me
yet me causing tension is quit impressive
but perhaps I don't want that anymore
I will float somewhere in between the two of those
because life never pulls us anywhere
our emotions always do
so that means that because of how I feel
I probably create feeling misunderstood

Crying boys

where do you belong?

novels upon novels
and none write my story
growth of different life forces
but none create a forest
a lot of different roads
a lot of different people
if only I was patient enough
I'm forcing our threads through the needles
novels upon novels
no characters like us
hereby, I write my own story
because I won't let boxes be a must

Crying boys

the ego is a temporary thing,
that can make absolute decisions

I deserve more credit than I received
and I decided this out of ego,
which means
I had the pride to believe it
but not the understanding that it's true
and even though I deserve it,
I had to learn to be humble
before receiving
what I deserved all along

birthing miracles

I am the greatness
I was seeking in others
I gave birth to miracles
not needing mothers

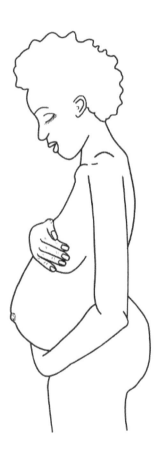

Crying boys

anxiety

it didn't happen today
it has already passed
yet somehow,
you put your memories to the test
it has not happened yet
but you draw it into your time
you already feel the heartache
and the stress through your spine
it didn't happen today
but your memories bring it here
it either already did or hasn't happened yet,
which counts for all your fears

Crying boys

roller coaster ride

you make me want to ride
every roller coaster in life
you make me want to breathe
and plant all the flower seeds
you make me want to grow
you make me want to know
you make me reach and dive
because of you I want to be alive

Crying boys

procrastination

today and tomorrow
you call them the same
acting like some action
will actually cause you pain
being repetitive and sensitive
making plans that are always tentative
you make me worried,
and now you are experiencing guilt
what about all these amazing things
that you have already built?
how do you ever get to your destination,
with all this unnecessary procrastination?

Crying boys

go for all you want

I'm not going to tell you
to let go of things
that obviously mean a lot to you
I know the world will tell you to let go
because that thing feels heavy on you
but no achievement is yours to have
until you make it so

I have a dream,
and I'm letting no one tell me
that I can't achieve it

Crying boys

admire your own gallery

process and progress is more art
than the final destination
the final destination
is just to frame it

death is also rebirth

I will break every part of me
I will cry out all my tears
I will destroy every emotion
I feel or have ever
just to never go through what I did
ever again
some might call it healing
and others might call it denial,
but all I know is that this destruction
is needed to ever create beauty again

Crying boys

dimensions of water

tell me how long does it take
to cross the ocean waves
to get where I was meant to be
the ~~better~~ greatest side was meant for me

Crying boys

I am

I ~~will be~~ am more wonderful
than the old me
could even have the imagination
to dream or think about

Crying boys

singing a duet

I'm the romance due to my own intensity
falling in love with pieces of minds
self image built on this duet
because my body and mind are singing
the voice of angels,
polished in a diamond mouthpiece
they belong together like honey and its bee
melodies that melt beautifully
and appear like chocolate on a hot summer day
singing a duet
that only great souls really hear
every tone kisses one another
making love with words as the vibrations are near
entering the eardrums
making all our hate numb
intensifying emotions
activating gently in the body
and it shines through our skin and eyes
confidence and self love is a blessing

Crying boys

self love

self love at its finest
I'm making my bed
laid by two
we are finding rest
can I do
what you did best?
I know I do
my love is more blessed

finding self love at its
finest
it does not compare
to what you gave
to make it truly flourish
I buried my concept
of love in a grave
I know you did
what I do now best

which is loving me

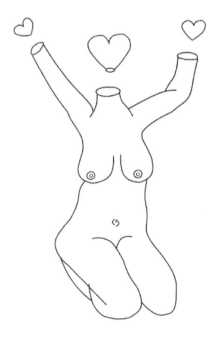

Crying boys

broken bones and spilled milk

I don't care what anybody says
I know what I want
and when I want it
I am fighter for it
regardless of my circumstances
I have broken bones for no reason
and cried over spilled milk
so I am very willing
to give my all
to achieve exactly what I want

Crying boys

why are you running?

running from the truth
it is not something you can hide
we meet rainbows when we realize
that the world isn't black and white

Crying boys

what is repetition?

someone is going to tell you
the exact things I am now,
and you will tell them
that they are crazy
so you will tell the next
and the next after that
until you declare everyone as being crazy
claiming you are the only one sane,
while your life will never feel complete
because you expect different results
while doing the same

what is insanity?

Crying boys

is it worth it?

not every argument
is worth getting angry over
or crying yourself to sleep for
not every argument
is even worth having
and no argument
is worth remembering
or keeping yourself awake for

Crying boys

resistance

I embrace
what I am feeling
please
don't push it away
it is okay
to feel some fire
because the rain
will wash it away

Crying boys

remember what you said

I know, it has been a while
but remember what you said
whatever you believe you deserve,
is always what you get
so I believe I deserve love,
abundance and feeling enough
and for whatever I put my mind to
I will always be qualified
I believe I attract happiness
and regardless of all the ups and downs,
I will end up satisfied

Crying boys

balance of life

you balance on a scale
of emotions and detachment
being who you want to be
and killing who you used to be
but when things get to be great
they also get to be awful
that's the balance of life

Crying boys

when it's good, it's great

when it's a high, it's great
but when it's low
it's real, real low
I guess thats what they call life
good things come and go
when it's good, it's well
and when it's bad, I feel odious
those are the pulls of the strings of life
that I call awfully incommodious

Crying boys

me telling myself to get over myself

the world is not ending
and when people treat you well
they're not pretending
every hurt is not a personal attack
and that you treat people well
doesn't guarantee they will do that back
and the way you love
is not how you will be loved
when people don't meet your expectations,
you don't have to feel crushed
every inconvenience shouldn't make you bitter,
and every tear doesn't have to turn into a river

Crying boys

emotions are in motion

never pay for anything in life
with your emotions
because emotions will then
control your life
when emotions are not under control
everything will go wrong
and you will be blinded from seeing
the things that do go right

Crying boys

mother of the temple

she gave birth in a temple
that she had created on her own
no man ever gave her a child
she has built her own throne
collected her diamonds, made her own crown
she lifts herself up whenever she is down
animals in the kingdom listen to her sounds
she births her own miracles and heals her own wounds
magic is alive in her life
she is the goddess that demands a sacrifice
but she is sun, storm, rain, good and bad
after every war she fights,
she flourishes in the aftermath

Crying boys

when minds dance

music to my eyes
beauty in my ears
sounds good to my hands
the wonders that no one hears
but everybody feels
everyone wants to know
how it feels when two minds dance
and keep dancing through all the lows
music to the mind
rhythm to the eyes
dancing in sync through the romantic highs

Crying boys

the lovers

deadly deeds, planted seeds
please grow vastly
absorb my greed
I need to know, I need to learn
the past in flames, just let it burn
the past in flames, don't touch my skin
before I commit a shameful sin
behold, the pain that makes us in love
only if we knew what that even was
oh the virus, I am infected
two hopeless souls, strongly connected
bones cracking
reshaping from vintage dust, oh I'm sore
saying my goodbyes
as I am not the same anymore

Crying boys

Crying boys

you are a priority

priorities are important
make sure that
what is a priority
always comes first
and always constantly treat yourself
like you're important
or else you won't be important
in your own life

Crying boys

craving the utmost

never ask yourself
for the bare minimum
you deserve to give yourself
the utmost
because life is already filled
with people who will tell you
that the bare minimum is too much,
and all the bare minimum will do
is make you crave something
you already have been told
you are not worthy of
limits are there
when we create them
and they go away
when we break them

Crying boys

answer the questions

I can taste the overthinking
like fresh pressed juice
in your morning mind
at night, it knows the taste
of the liquor of your emotional side
perhaps, that is just you experiencing
a hangover of your mistakes
answer all the questions to yourself honestly
and maybe you will know
how liberation really tastes

Crying boys

the greatest

you have created in being
so many wonderful things
you are the author
of both your physical realm
and your mental plane
no destinies that decide
where you go
you have birthed this greatnesses,
and you are the star of this show

Crying boys

no limits in sight

be honest to yourself,
and please learn self acceptance
learn the art of self understanding
love yourself more than anyone can ever do
discipline your mind, but please be kind
but after mastering these things,
there will be absolutely nothing
you can't achieve

Crying boys

crying in mirror

love me
please love me
because without your love
I love different

love me
please love me

I usually don't beg
but I figured begging a mirror
is not that bad

divine nature

divinity.
the word that is a poem by itself

out of this world
sounding out of my reach

yet I know that it is beautiful

Crying boys

Chapter Two

Dark Imagination

Crying boys

wired

you enhance everything you touch
the good and the bad
you are always doing too much
the good and the bad
nobody appreciates your rectitude,
but people you have shown righteousness to
remember you as a nuisance
tying you with powerless wires
making you feel like all the weight is on you
the more you fight it
the more it hurts
while all you had were good intentions

freed from the wires
wearing scars, reminding you of the pain
and it's a sin to think
that they created a beast
now it's shameful to be hateful
so instead of blaming them
you start using wires yourself
restricting them from hurting you
and now you being the bad guy
is strangely absurd to you

Crying boys

you get to be a stranger

you were important to who I was
but you are a stranger to who I am

Crying boys

higher being

maybe there are no saviors,
but only creators

Crying boys

I get to be art

they say art is supposed to make you
feel something
not necessarily be pleasing to the eyes
and maybe that is right
because all art I have experienced
wasn't comprehensible to the eyes
It awakened new worlds in my mind

Crying boys

mind

I learned my lesson
this time I will lose myself
before I lose you
because you can build me up
but I can't build you up
and eventually I need you to teach me
how to built you up

Crying boys

tomorrow, when today is over

there are only todays, and laters
no yesterdays or tomorrows
there are reasons to have
and reasons to will
but only in the exception of now,
there is no melancholy or destiny
there is only our lack of understanding
and our simple egoistic self in the way
there is no forceful manipulation
our consciousness just surrenders
there is no middle road
just one road in the middle,
and the side roads are there just for the view
the impression of free will is what it is
there is no unsteadiness, there is off course
there are no escape routes,
just rooms that make things worse
there is no drunken or high truth,
just the reality of being sober
and sometimes, there is time
tomorrow, when today is over

Crying boys

saving poison

one of the greatest gifts
to give yourself
is the balance between
emotions and detachment
outer perspective and humanity
on a balanced scale

but no one in this story
was every worried about bearing gifts
everyone in this story
was worried about saving
the poison of it all
- the ego

Crying boys

why do I not want to feel?

it's the most honest and direct question
I ever asked myself
it's not about whether feeling is good or bad
it's about vulnerability
and my shame towards it
it's my reluctancy towards vulnerability
I have learned how not to feel shameful
about anything
but I guess vulnerability is my vulnerability
because it's the only fragile thing about me
do I feel shame admitting this?
I don't really do, I suppose
but it feels like taking one piece of clothing off
at a time
and showing something underneath
that even I haven't looked at in a while
which is me, but we are strangers
we just act like the both of us don't exist
and the confrontation of the reflection we denied
both hits us with feelings
and feelings lead to emotions
and emotions, lead to motions,
which mostly will end up hurting
and make me feel even more

Crying boys

black-out

the reason that he is still alive
is finding the art of black-out poetry
he blacked out parts of his life
and leaves open what he wants to see
because all that has been blacked out
is too dark to read

Crying boys

the darkness

I felt fine with my eyes closed
knowing my heart was beating just for me
letting go of all the petty nerves
I can give myself exactly what I need
I felt hesitant about sleeping early
most of the time the day starts at night
I felt fine with my eyes closed
getting comfortably without the light
and the stars were hugging me
the planets were bugging me
they told me that no goal can be too far,
and if I reach I won't ever fall that hard
but I ended up falling asleep
under my favorite comfortable sheets
going over all my desires, wishes and needs
and in the morning when waking up
the birds sang my song
it was a song only I could hear,
which I probably knew all along
I was rising up like the bright morning sun
as the stars faded with dazzling light
whoever said,
what goes up, must come down,
must have been right

Crying boys

most evil of them all

in this story,
there are no princesses, no frogs
and no princes or towers
just a bunch of villains fighting
over who is the most evil
of them all

so if you have to question
if you are the bad guy
then you probably are

Crying boys

impulsive behavior is flammable

anger liquidates like gasoline
has been thrown upon the fire
burning down every will to live
breaking relationships and desires
burning the flesh, creating restrictions
feeding veins like an addiction
hoping my enmity
won't make my choices
hoping I can extinguish
these hostile voices
I hope you understand
I am still the person
you currently miss
I just caught fire
and I never meant to
burn like this

Crying boys

**I don't want revenge, I want reparation
(and sometimes that's revenge)**

a curse cast on the heartbreakers
may be solace for the broken hearts
the cuts and bruises in their skin
may be reparation for broken parts
may I feel, may I know
what caused life to turn to stone
for this one time, we all trade our roles
I play the devil,
you play the vulnerable souls
I will make you feel
all I once knew
and all the cuts I will be causing
will be left for you to sew
like a puppet stuck in a play
doing whatever I desire and whatever I say
and then I look in the mirror
seeing the previous stories fade
we will all be happier
playing out this scene my way

Crying boys

cold

you loved so much
because you didn't know how to hate
then a sudden storm
made everything deteriorate
the pain in you
called your mind,
and told you that being hateful
is the same as being kind
now you hate so much
and you love even more
you're turning into someone cold,
and all the goodness in you now feels unsure

Crying boys

pretty lies and the ugly truth

mind you, I am at war
and fighting back only gets you so far
shining in the dark doesn't make you a star
and breaking slightly or hard
are both still falling apart
the sound of breaking is a sign
you still got a heart to break
begging for peace doesn't mean a truce
and you won't grow if hearing the truth
is what you refuse

Crying boys

gatekeepers

pouring drinks
or straight out of the bottle
mourning our hearts
and spreading their gospel
admiring the presence
in the creation from vibes
the law of dismissing grudges
left to be solved for other nights
can I pray like a mail order?
the bottles probably went over borders
I just need a hand
I can't pretend
that I didn't share drinks,
with problem solvers

Crying boys

oxytocine

the air gets radioactive
when we are together
and if you were a person
it would be easy
because I could tell you to go away,
which is funny
because I never told someone to go
but no, you are not human,
so I can't desire for a pain to cause
and even if I could
I would never get that far
because I would miss you so much
but your poison has caused me losses,
and I don't know if I'm willing
to lose more or to lose you

Crying boys

people forget you,
because you barely remember yourself

death is sometimes not something you are
sometimes it's something you feel
and if you feel something long enough,
you become it
more than once or twice
I felt them
and just before I reached climax
I let go every time
and so we go
having a love-hate relationship
and always having each other
at the backs of our minds

Crying boys

Crying boys

when I dream

we share a screen and so many places
we live and talk in so many spaces
looking in the mirror
and the more there are
dimensions truly don't exist that far
every time I go
I have this little saying
every true desire is worth a little waiting
off I go, in the screen of dreams
they could never be too big it seems
people die, some stay alive
I died too or maybe I survived
I can't really know
because people play the show
every time I dream
off I go
jumping and destroying
destruction is my creation
dreams made in my head
meeting lands and welcoming nations
creating my own greener side
I promise that is my destination
it came from somewhere whenever I dream
this is the front of my dark imagination

Crying boys

when I finally fall asleep

the first sinking, do you know?
consciousness fading, now I go
hands relaxing really slow
I am already gone for all I know

the creature of the dark
no name, no actions she takes
she gives me her power
I create until the moment I wake
move, speak, touch, love, hate
at my command it all has to be made
speed, words, borders and gates
when I feel, and when I say
maybe it's an escape I seek
that I only get whenever I sleep

Crying boys

even far away, close we'll be

we will get there
whatever it takes
from rocky mountains
to stormy waves
from broken paths
you will receive my message
no obstacle is invincible
we will have safe passage

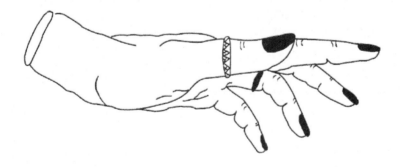

Crying boys

only as alive as me

in need of you to make amends
we were never bad at reinventions
you are not well nor alright
showing me you are sorry with attention
I made you see, you made me blind
now you're blind, and I can see
how I stayed awake loving myself
is now how you stay awake
just loving me

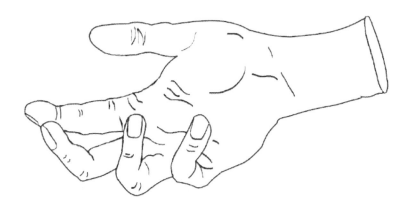

Crying boys

lucid

you are the movement of the water
I'm blowing bubbles
that then softly fill my lungs
now your streams move a little faster
I'm not resisting
we taste the salt on our tongues
our touch is getting lucid
I guess that happens
when our hearts beat in sync
our eyes get to meet omissions
we are stuck living in my dreams,
and I want neither of us to blink

Crying boys

the opposite

days and nights
the wrongs, the rights
black and white
the peace and fights
the love and hate
it's all the same
it's all different
but all imitate

Crying boys

insomnia

I am tired of being tired
I just really want to sleep
it has been over 48 hours
I am not capable of counting sheep
I slowly start to hallucinate
fragments that might be real
friendly poison is being injected into me
but I won't ever make that a big deal
can I please close my eyes?
and actually fall asleep?
all these restless imaginations
are for my dreams to keep

Crying boys

the living

I have died more times
than I have been alive
so you can kill my spirit
as much as you want
but I have already
seen the other side

Crying boys

I bought a shovel

you don't hate me
you don't have to pretend
both you and me
know that I'm heaven sent
It's 3 am, I crave a cigarette
I'm out with a shovel
meeting my friends
we bury some stuff,
we bury some love
the moon is down here
and also above
I know it's dangerous outside
for a young girl like me
but I already plan
on saving me

Crying boys

only around to hurt

did it hurt
when you climbed up from hell?
around here
nobody has a soul to sell
we have hearts
but they belong to our other parts
which weren't even ours
from the start
but did it hurt,
when you climbed up from hell?
I can bet you will like this place
very well
we got heartless people, and dark desires
and plenty of love to sell

Crying boys

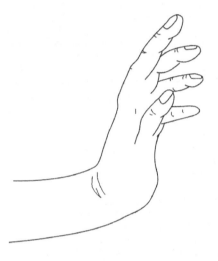

people feel lonely

the rhythm held by fire
I refuse to feel alone
is it bad to ask for company?
I miss the warmth in every bone
this, I have never known
tears have made me stoop this low
feelings have no way out
because I can't cry anymore
all I pour is fire
from rhythm on my own
I will turn into the flame itself
so I will no longer feel alone
this way, I can keep myself warm
people get lonely
when left with empty arms

Crying boys

matter

burnings in my chest
that feels like the entire world
is being pushed unto me
and the darkness is so bright
it makes me forget
what living actually feels like
it makes me forget about humanity
mundane laws and the concept of time
it whispers
I still see you
the importance of you, the goddess
you matter and so does your vessel
your aspirations and your effort
you just don't live in here
and now it's time to get out,
so please open your eyes
and live life as it's known
as the best version of yourself

Crying boys

the mess you made

look at all the messy things
you do, and say
you're just like glitter,
once touched
you're all over the place

Crying boys

unworthy and empty

jokes and laughter
please laugh, it's all a joke
emptiness is never that serious
until feeling fulfilled goes up in smoke
and the ashes don't even taste that bitter
until it gets in your lungs and you choke
now you are uncertain
of the unworthiness you have invoked
but to taste happiness again
these are all tastes that have to be let go off
to ever touch love again
you have to embrace the emptiness,
and that will mean space for all the love
who knew there was use for all that space?
space that wakens a new phenomenon
called contentment,
which feels and smells better
than the air in your emptiness

Crying boys

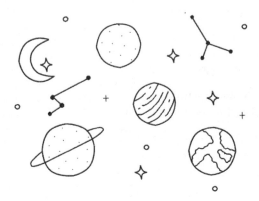

the waning moon

you are the reason
why the moon is currently waning
turning the universe into a trans
for the human mind to feel like intoxication
feeding off the energies floating
like dust particles
has something ever felt so draining?
I can't let that slide, like a broken dam
I will make all your bad actions drown
until we reach the new moon again

Crying boys

I'm sorry that I'm not sorry

I'm not going to apologize
for the way I am healing
and I'm not apologizing
for the way I broke myself,
just to put you together
I'm not apologizing for the person I am now,
because of how I broke
I'm not apologizing for my strength
because it's the reason I'm still alive
and just because I'm strong
doesn't mean you get to take advantage of that
by breaking me some more,
just because I can handle that
I'm not going to allow you
to pull the ground from under my feet
you're not getting an apology
for me simply being me

Crying boys

happiness happens

I don't want you to happen
I want us to happen
but right now
I feel like you don't know
what is happening
and that happens to be
what has to happen
for us to be happy

Crying boys

truthful

tell me when you are ready to be honest
because I always was
but also tell me when you are ready
to actually hear the truth

Crying boys

forget about it

can you still remember?
the promise of December?
forget about it
I don't need no new years resolutions
worries of time becoming diminutions
promises are boring
because I take them seriously
I should really get over that
I'm too old for pinky promises
I am just the right age
for old school self medication
and instead of forgetting about it
I text while drunk or high yet staying awake
forgetting is so boring
let's feel the burden and feel the regret
until we drown in sorrows we can't forget
now all we got is ashes and empty cups
I guess growing up really sucks

Crying boys

I want to do what you did to me

just a random thought
let's remember broken hearts
kind of in that mood, it's kind of goals
to have a collection of stolen souls,
and there is this one special one
I want to break
just to keep
and when it cries and begs me
I tell it what has been told to me
that there is no need to cry
you're overreacting
it's really not that
deep

Crying boys

cursed they be

a knife cutting the skin
that I know it hurts
but who would've thought
it would never compare
to cruel minds planning death
leaving innocents in despair
if I could make the choice once again
it may go to war with the surface of my skin
make me pour out all my ingratitude
and confess my darkest sins
but what my mind created
while I was gone
is not created from right or wrong

Crying boys

I could never do what you did

I intend your heart to break
like my heart did,
when my love was all yours to take
I hope the thought alone
of oxygen
entering your lungs,
will extinguish every light you know
I pray your conscious demands repentance
that you will be barely able to endure
all that you made me feel
is what will hurt your own feelings now
I know for sure
I desire this to be the only way
that you will ever find happiness again
because I refuse to believe
that you get to take mine
and get to live all happy and fine

Crying boys

if you do, I do it too-those are the rules

I don't have to touch you
to know that you touch me
because whether you are here or there
in my mind, you are everywhere
and knowing me,
I will allow it to spread like a disease
I promise I will touch you too
until you get contaminated
and I am all over you

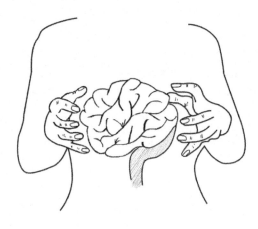

Crying boys

deadly feelings

understand my roads
I went off course not so long ago,
but I control the weather
as you know
but I got better
don't you know?
I am completely healed
doesn't it show?
I met the stars and sun
don't I glow?
you saw my worst, but I promise
I will never again stoop so low
to hell I went
blame it on our feelings
they come but never go
we felt deadly feelings,
I already told you so

Crying boys

I am a handful for my own hands

I limit my consuming of art
because I want to prevent
meeting more versions of me
than I already know,
yet I love to see other people
meeting new versions of themselves
now I hope I can introduce you
to a version you didn't know

Crying boys

a poem to my mind

I can't afford to lose you
you are all I have
I can't afford to lose you
you're the one that knows me best
I can't afford to think
that this might be all a test
I can't afford to lose you
and that is really all I know
is "too late to say sorry" a thing?
maybe, I lost you long ago

Crying boys

friends and lovers

I wanted to fall asleep
under lilac skies
because they remind me of
our psychedelic nights
our gentle sins,
our aggressive bond
oh, look at all the body parts
we have wronged
the brain, the heart, the lips,
the hands
can you believe they are lovers?
when they once were just friends?
and yes, that is wrong
this love is so precarious
because it's not romantic,
like most lovers
it's selfish and imperious

Crying boys

naked thoughts

you are the poetic, making me a poet
pouring thoughts on every note
is my mind allowed to ever dress?
you drown what I try to keep afloat
feelings don't get the same nudity
all of a sudden she's a whore
you beating on her like a drum
now she is making dirt all over the floor
who is cleaning up this mess?
perhaps, the both of us are to blame
but I will be the bigger person
although I don't know how to hide the stains
feelings don't get the same nudity
all of a sudden, she's a whore
we can't give her a sky of clouds
because she always turns into a storm

Crying boys

needing to be in control

you are the map of making wonders
I read your borders like a book
you have created all these places
eye-catching,
I don't know where to look
I'm the immigrant to your land
visiting all your dangerous seas
I belong is what I pretend
I'm confident while making guarantees
you have created all these places
everyone just plays their part in this art
it's quit upsetting that being in control
is the only thing keeping you
from falling apart

Crying boys

nightmares

they say
you can't fully see
until you close your eyes
so I did and saw a screen of black
making sound in my ears
warning me about storms
that were yet to come,
but I wasn't afraid
because not every storm
washes away the beautiful
some cleanse all that hurts

Crying boys

broken records on repeat
static songs played about me
how amazing I am, but how boring I get
and how every inconvenience
is seen as a threat
static, static, it hurts my ears
confronting me about all my fears
I have to buy a new record player
and play a new song
old patterns, the same old song
literally and metaphorically
that is why everything goes wrong
I know what to do, I know what I should know
So please explain to me,
why I don't do so

I bought a new record player,
but I still play the same song
I guess I am strong
but not strong enough to let go
this one looks better
but of course it sounds the same
because it's the same old record
it's not as big a change as I claimed

the scrappy record will ruin my new player
the record itself is damaged
layer upon layer
it's time to take it out
and see what real change is all about

Crying boys

the price of happiness

I got a pain and it's called happiness
all I wished for and still this emptiness
nothing to fill up, it's just a hole
I don't want to fall in it and lose my soul
I got a pain, and it's called drugs
sold my light for a couple bucks
now was it really worth it?
I will buy another one, that looks new,
since I can afford to

Crying boys

black hole

cosmic voices tell me you need me
fire fighting fire, you complete me
I don't hurt, only if you let me
I don't want to lose us
you are the only one that gets me
together we could adjust the entire milky way
because soul connections
are that strong, they say
I want you to float in my galaxy
until all you hear is static
make love with all my atoms
until you experience all my magic
just to find out we never had a soul
I want you and me
to be sucked into a black hole

Crying boys

Chapter Three

Patience

Crying boys

the law of trust

trust is not a feeling
a saying or a thought
it is to know
and to trust means to be patient
because you know it will come
you know it will happen
and it sure will stay,
especially when it has proven
it won't leave
sometime before

Crying boys

a prayer

I make every second count
set intentions without a doubt
make it clear, let it go
making all fruitions easily flow
time is running out
I don't get what all these rules are about
I want to decide when things come in
and also when they come out
but we live by the rules
of a void beyond the stars
the galaxy and its divinity
and all its supernatural parts
its femininity and masculinity
and all the energy we assume
to flow
the whole entire experience
feels like one joke of a show

Crying boys

all the pain I have put you through

I know soon you will tell me
about all stories that happened in hell
you will look me in the eyes and tell me
about the hole that you fell into
you will shrug away the trauma
and tell me about how hurt you used to be
you will tell me about your friendship with the devil
and the light you learned to see
you will then act like you never mentioned the devil
and then your eyes will start to water
you will then scoff away the pain and tell me
you don't understand why you ever bothered
the watery eyes then disappear ,
and all emotions vanish into the void
I will then understand you did this all
just to attract crying boys

Crying boys

creating tomorrow

detach, let go
tomorrow is a thought
and not known

Crying boys

no consequences for hurting me

moved by words
without movement
because words are only alive
when he gave them a heartbeat
he might be a serial killer,
he sweeps words off their feet
moved by time
only when it stays still
he feels the time different
after a couple of pills,
makes his every tear
turn into someone else's pain
and all his happiness
he keeps for himself
moved by how he moves
he doesn't care to change,
and why would he
if he can move whatever he wants
and will always get it back

Crying boys

haunting venom

I fixed my mouth
because it was speaking venom
the serpent of my voice was hissing,
and I wished it to be soft like spun wool
but it just bites every prey it catches
I fixed my words
cause they were haunting
feeling hunger for a fresh catch,
and when it doesn't get feed
all hell breaks loose
maybe they just can't
help themselves

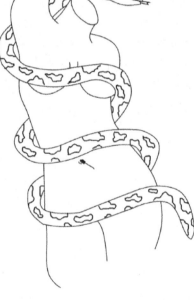

Crying boys

learning to create time

materialization of patience
seen by eyes through the art of time
the prince of all powers
killing everything that feels nice
the word goes around
that time actually does not exist,
which will never be a bandaid
to all the good times that I have missed

Crying boys

404 not found

the annihilation of our universe
is blooming across our qualms
we are searching for solutions,
while the answer is in our palms
we see forgiveness like an individual
we are forced to be around
and let go of all past grudges or our humanity
will be nowhere to be found

Crying boys

nothing is fixed

don't resist
the glimpse of freedom
all that is said and done
I know you can heal them

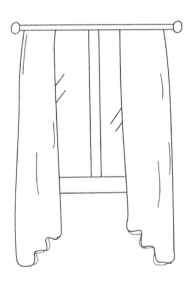

Crying boys

appointed hour

the longing of the pen
to reach paper to create
not simple fiction stories
but future and a fate
the mind working through the hours
makes me think I'm wasting time
I know patience is important,
but I keep looking for the signs
but now I will remember
because remembering is reality
I will not let these impatient tenancies
get the best of me

Crying boys

doctor, please listen

I have a wound,
and it's called impatience
and it contains an infection called time
it might be a part of a diagnosis
that I right now can't define
the wound won't close
you know how that feels?
and I might be my own doctor
who now has to make me heal

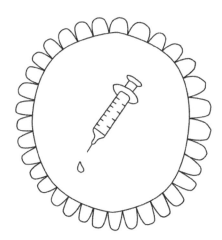

sad angels

poor guardian angel
has to do a lot of saving
coping mechanisms and complications
he is busy
with the way I have been behaving
he has cut off his wings
and fell down on earth
feeling rage towards me
because of all the feelings I have hurt
including mine, but that got less painful
over time
by now, he probably feels like he is wasting time
poor guardian angel
don't feel burdened,
I have changed my ways
now I hope it pays off
within a couple of days

Crying boys

Father, may I water?

I watered the plants
five times a day
because I was eager for them to grow
little did I know
I was drowning the seeds,
that were trying so hard
to grow roots for me
but without roots,
there won't be fruits
next time,
more patient I will be

Crying boys

what is refused attention doesn't grow

it's not worth the effort
it's not worth the emotions
the time or even the understanding
it's not worth the risk
if you love yourself,
and if you truly know
the end result won't serve you
don't serve it your attention
let it go
because tomorrow it will manifest
it's nonexistence
like it never caused turmoil in the first place

Crying boys

I bought the lemons life gave to me myself

happiness lives here
in the garden of games
and satisfaction plays a bigger role,
but let's not name by names
I accept the fact that delay
is all made by my mind
but I have never really been the one
to gracefully handle time,
but I am now the one
who flows to where I want to go
patience just might be the key
I missed for all I know

Crying boys

knowledge without borders

I'm sure both of us will cross waves
that will be nothing compared
to the salty oceans
that have touched our skin
but I know how to swim,
and I'm very sure you don't
because people who don't want to learn,
don't get to know

Crying boys

you still have time

stop now
before you end up in a place
from which you will have no idea
how to get yourself out
stop now
before you cause wounds
that will leave scars
that will make you keep remembering
what you did
change
before there will be no chance to,
and everything has to be replaced
throw all cards on the table
because you don't want to come to the realization
when all is to ashes, and it's too late

Crying boys

the evil second

I don't want to meet you half way
I just expect you to do everything I say
everything I wish at my command
I might sound selfish,
based on most peoples assessment
but every second counts,
and I don't like to wait
I don't walk the roads, if it ain't my way,
and I don't know if I'm right to do that
or whether I should really change my ways,
but every second counts
and time doesn't wait for me
my impatience probably caused
time to grow hate for me

Crying boys

mountains

I know patience
will get me to climb mountains
and see the overall view
while watching over all that is yet to come
and all I wish I knew
I know patience
will get me on rooftops
and see skylines I used to dream about
if only I made it that easy
for me to reach the clouds

Crying boys

I have never been so happily unhappy

life is getting greater
creation is the start I see
fulfilling wishes like a bottled genie
I'm juggling all parts of me
I can't seem to worry,
to feel bad, or feel alarmed
have I already mentioned
how creation can cause harm?
maybe that is my intention
because my happiness
won't be everyone's reflection
what will bother my satisfaction?
I can't wait now to shine later
the end result is all I see
this is who I want to be

accountability

nobody can be as in my head as I can
nobody is whispering for me to make mistakes
to be angry or impatient
all there is is my mind, my action,
and me to take accountability for it
admit my wrongs, even I need to hear a
"I told you so" sometimes in return
whatever it takes,
whatever it breaks
to learn all the lessons that need to be learned
for my own sake

Crying boys

uncomfortable

you're so uncomfortable with change
that you'd rather poison yourself with the past
while wondering why the present hurts so much
you're so uncomfortable with time
that you never enjoy what is now
and end up poisoning every memory
you are so sad about who you was
that who you are
gives you so much adrenaline,
causing you to be your own high,
and that is a good thing but it can get bad
when you get lost in being high
you're so comfortable with your perspectives
that grasping the existence of other minds
is such an unfortunate concept to you,
but change is okay and so are memories,
loving yourself is amazing
and accepting that not everybody
experiences the same things like you
is less normal to you than it should be

Crying boys

it's not that bad

remember that it's not that deep
not that bad,
not that personal
and not that serious
as you are right now making it out to be

Crying boys

bored

please be like me
me being you is getting boring
why are you creating leaves?
and why am I creating trees?
when we could create a forest?

Crying boys

altered

she has this idea that comfort lies in me
I guess we always seek comfort
in uncomfortable places
because comfortable ones are already
what we want them to be,
and I get greedy in being the most comfortable
I guess that is why she is seeking me,
but greedy people
have many losses
and so did she, seeking me,
so we altered our states of being
losing comfort and losing needs
which hurts a lot, it breaks you apart
to not be allowed to need comfort,
but I suppose needing is greedy,
and being greedy is uncomfortable

Crying boys

meeting again

for all we know,
we are each other's time machines
because every time we see each other
we meet again,
and love again,
but I never fall in love
because just like time
in this time machine, love doesn't exist
all affection just lasts forever

redemption and recovery

they say
seek and you shall find,
so I went wandering
for my mind,
and I found him
near disaster
I wish I had found him faster,
and when I reached
they merged into one
like two liquids in a pot
to be extracted
or embraced and loved
if you don't get better,
you will be judged
to be patient and extract
recovery at its best

Crying boys

be well soon

the beatings of a whip
it's scarring up my mind
speedy healing, it stopped bleeding
is this what they call a sign?
mourning for the dead skin
falling off like petals on a wilting flower
do you mind forgetting time?
stop counting growth by the hour

I get back when I get back
I am healing, I promise you that
we don't get to take back what we said
because at the time it was all we meant

the beatings of a whip
it has scarred how you look in the mirror
I don't mind if you cry
tears might even make things clearer
mourning the choices you made
it's clear you know better now
but we can't know without the lows,
so some turmoil has to be allowed

Crying boys

patience

some things take time
get over it
or stay on it,
and watch it get you by

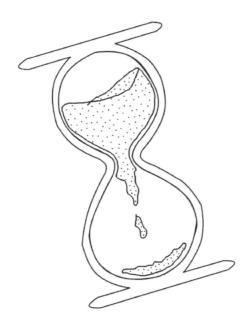

Crying boys

to my mind, please be kind

it's 3.00 am
you're not being loud
just being crowding
I don't know what it's about,
maybe if you stop controlling me
I can learn to take control
maybe if we got along better
I would have a calmer soul

Crying boys

healing

I promise you
I heard you the first time
the second time,
the third time
and the fourth time
when you
yelled
and yelling
over and over
does not compel me
I'm healing on my own time,
and doing that carefully
is not a crime

Crying boys

watch me flow

I'm melting,
molding into whatever I want to be
because I can feel the rush
of how powerful I am
I feel charged by an energy
I have craved for so long,
and I always want my world
to reflect, what I feel
I'm melting, which makes me flow
I can go wherever I want to go
which makes me able to be
whatever, whenever
no limits I can see

Crying boys

all is given to you

the kingdom is not a neighbor
I found embedded in bible verses
may I find that power in my own savior
but who is preventing him from casting curses?
I was already saved from drowning
in waters that offered me absolution
burning salty lungs might be what felt arousing
resuscitated, but returned to a life of convolution
I have become life to a state of even being grateful
intending worshippers to be faithful
is being faithful our choice?
conversations with saviors, is that my own voice?

Crying boys

impatient

I know you only mean well,
but good intentions
can harm too
I calm
all your breakdowns,
but when you get inpatient,
there is nothing I can do

Crying boys

I deserve all I want

I lost because
I have put all I love on a pedestal
but I should consider those things normal
because I truly am enough
and if I don't believe that
or if there is a breath crumb of doubt
I will continue telling myself
that I am more than enough
until I believe it, not a little bit
but more than enough

Crying boys

worth the pain

paradise is found
in your calming breathing sounds
time has passed and already caused
the strength for healing wounds
this love's tranquility
made every second in pain count

Crying boys

until love do us apart

there is no aftermath,
there is no end
all there is
is now
and us
and all kinds of feelings
that if it was up to me
are allowed to live till eternity
please don't let go
don't open your eyes
In the race of life,
you are my prize

Crying boys

author

retracing stories
with low-budget schemes
rewriting scenarios
making award-winning scenes

Crying boys

just do it already

doubt might be an insult to yourself
because you only ever want
the best for yourself,
and if you truly believe that
there will be no place for doubt
every journey will be wonderful
the small and the long ones
the rocky roads and the easy flows

Crying boys

my mind is a greater artist than I have ever been

I promised my hands they will touch
all that my mind molds to reality
from my satisfaction of happiness
to your everlasting love
may I taste the cold of water
on hot summer days
where we feel each other's skin
kissing sun rays
until we know our minds will melt
like ice cubes
together like we always would

Crying boys

all the things we should've done

we should've bought more flowers
we should've committed more crimes
we should've talked more about our feelings,
and we should've yelled at each other less
we should've told more jokes,
and we should've had more laughs
we should've been more honest,
and we should've given each other our best
we should've done a lot of things
like die more and live less
because only if we let parts die
we can live away from all this mess
but there is still time,
that must be a sign
that we can still do
all that we should
have done
maybe we actually
killed our old
beings,
and life has just
begun

Crying boys

too busy for time

well look at you,
your confidence is looking glorious
your success is quit notorious
feeling like the world is at your feet
getting all you want and all you need
keeping yourself busy
with loving yourself and being loved
being humble is not that hard
but look at you, all is in your hand,
even better than you had planned
you wear success like it's a part of you
attractiveness is even in the least of you

Crying boys

Chapter Four

Crying Boys

Crying boys

you don't get me anymore

we were born together
you were there
from the moment I came out of the womb
you gave life when I killed myself,
and you cheered on when I loved myself
you threw out you wings when I jumped,
and you shook your head when I became
something I could only dream of
but you don't know about dreams,
do you?
because there is no moment that you sleep
there is no moment that you rest
am I what they call a liability?
I hate that word, it sounds so bad
never mind, forget I asked
I know you are probably now judging me
I didn't end up being the way I said I would be,
but don't lose me now
just because I changed to this
perhaps, we shouldn't be strangers now
I should find a way to understand you
now that you don't get me anymore
it's okay to admit
I am a mistake that you try to ignore

Crying boys

writing is being naked,
and maybe I don't know how to dress

I write poetry
to get over me
because I make such a big deal
out of every little itty bitty thing that I feel
I don't know where they come from
but I will continue until I'm numb

Crying boys

renaissance

brushes don't make paintings
our minds always have,
and words don't create peace
our love always has
and ocean waters don't get quiet
perhaps, you are the still water
of the rivers now
because all you made me feel
the good and the bad
has watered my garden of art,
which is unfortunate yet beautiful
at the same time
maybe,
you enhanced the quality of
my poetry

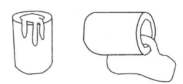

Crying boys

honesty is a lie

you asked me to be honest
and so I was
but for you, the truth was always too much
and calling me a liar
was much easier
but doing so couldn't kill the truth
telling the world I was a liar
was the only thing
that could make you feel good

Crying boys

gentle yet painful

love is not just a word
it's something you tell yourself
you are able to feel
your love hits me like a sword
the sharpening of the blade
is something that is such a big deal
am I even able to feel?
your cuts felt real to me
like a gentle, playful knife,
but I bleed like you have hit a vein
but your love,
has most definitely hit some nerves
Lord, who knew a lover could get so angry
with some misunderstood words?
I am bleeding to death
luckily sharp objects aren't allowed in heaven,
but I will write you a letter
from where I am
until your sharp corners get much softer

Crying boys

sacrifices out of love

I remember you told me
no matter how hard life gets
you would hold me,
but that was before I died
and you would have to make offers
to get here to the other side

- you don't meet the expectations of the new me

Crying boys

shattering our safe space

the shattering of your truth
was the most destructive lie
that has ever existed
breaking everything around us
but having mercy on the ego
turning my skin
into a target
catching every bullet being shot
the gunpowder is in the air
while we breathe it in
making our minds catch fire

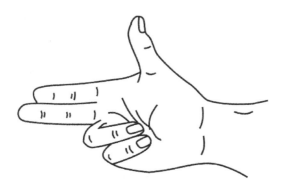

Crying boys

all is forgiven

I forgive me
because I can't forgive
all that is connected to me
if I hold grudges
against those on the exterior

Crying boys

what you wanted me to know

you know what is absolutely stupid?

the fact that I did so much soul searching
and fell in love with myself,
just to end up even more angry
because now I understood even less
why you don't see what I do

Crying boys

love is just a word

loving you is just a reckless
scientific experiment
while wearing no safety gear
just mixing up chemicals
burning skin,
damaging sight
and when everything is catching fire,
we both wonder what went wrong

Crying boys

adolescence

empty hands,
bad choices of friends
good people causing chaos
bad people wearing halos,
but we are better people now
rich hands
and classy one-night stands
no romance, just sad phone calls in bed
cold hands, we can't play tunes
unless it's our own horns that we toot
all other sounds are left on mute
warm hands,
and my poor wasted youth,
nobody will hurt me with this
attitude

Crying boys

the killer of joy

do you hear
the sound of pain?
it's pouring down like summer rain,
and do you know
the love I feel?
if only that was a feeling you could steal,
but you only steal happiness
not my feelings of sad teenage love,
you leave no physical evidence,
but in my mind you litter
now I guess I'm too grown
to lie you didn't
hurt me, and made me a little bitter

Crying boys

sorry is not a bad word

I don't want to use big words
with you now,
but I will tell you the biggest
of them all
I'm sorry
for thinking
that me lying to myself
was more important
than your feelings

                                        after all.

Crying boys

I don't get to treat you like you treat me

forgive me for being me
and forgive me for being you
being you is only a problem
when it's reflected in me
because you don't have a problem
with being you and making me feel it
but that is only if I'm being you
then the character is something to deal with

Crying boys

when I say sorry, I'm a better me

you keep my memories alive
and my forgetting of the past
is killing your memories
because all we have is the present now
we see scars and beliefs
that we gained during a life
we do not currently remember
but is carrying us
on all that currently keeps us alive
maybe that is because we died,
or maybe because the past has been revised

Crying boys

**even if I changed
I would still make the same mistakes**

I should've given you a warning
but warnings don't stop teenage boys
now we are adults,
but adults do whatever they want anyway
I should've been warned,
not that I would've listened anyway
a warning doesn't stop a loving heart,
so the story would've been the same

Crying boys

it's wrong but feels so good

you treated love as the most repulsive
of all human emotions
your pride was what you
had to carry
into every relationship you encountered
and admitting that you do love
was something that you only
wanted to understand
when you took that away
from the only one who cared
but you are still a human first
before you are a boy
so you too want love
it doesn't matter if it's fake
as long as it feeds your pride
like a Christmas feast
you hate, hate it so much
but just like most guilty pleasures,
 you keep coming back for more

Crying boys

taking control

you are a switch
that I can't control
when to turn on or off
but it's a switch that controls
when I shine or when I dim

I don't want you to be
the reason why I'm happy
because you are a condition
my happiness does not deserve

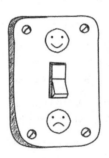

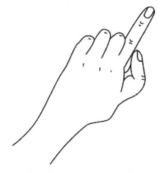

Crying boys

the sky has a friend

worrying clouds
cry to release stress
maybe we are in a competition
to see who can cry best
who can break their own heart
make their mind fall apart
who is the best at pushing blessings away
and self-sabotage
who is best at meeting bad people
who is worse at letting people in?
all this means that I have to say
that this is a competition I don't want to win

Crying boys

bad girls

self-growth,
required meeting crying boys
and very evil girls
it was the only way
I could ever learn
that they both exist in this world
hand in hand
hurting and loving

Crying boys

maybe you are sick

the ego is a symptom
of an illness called pride,
and sometimes we get symptoms
without ever being diagnosed

I need me to heal me
I need me
and I need to heal

Crying boys

cry, boy

you were the simplicity
I called love,
yet you are the most
complicated person I know,
but somehow, you made a way
to make me love you so much
it became too complicated for me
the only way to release that
was to let you go,
which was so simple
because that is
all boys like me know

but that was lying to myself
and what I felt then
will now never go

Crying boys

hands behind your head

you are trespassing in my mind
like a burglar
but the day and night
don't make any difference to you
getting caught or getting away
is not a worry that you face
sure, it crosses your mind,
but not like you are crossing mine
trespassing the concept
of what I get to feel and when I get to live
leaving your fingerprints everywhere
there is no spot that you miss

Crying boys

**I mean so much to you,
and that is sad but it's true**

then you cried
until crying was pondering through your head
hit with a shovel
in the back of your head
then you fell
in an already dug grave
bury your tears, and bury your hate

"baby, I can't keep being mad at you.
I don't want to lose us, and what I had
 with you."

Crying boys

ripe fruits

you are the sweetest cherry
in the bowl I have filled
I didn't want to taste any other,
and waste the affection that we have built
I hate every person judging us
for the theatrical act we have shown
I might plant a cherry tree,
grow sweet cherries on my own
I don't want us to overthink,
to remember or recall
I just want to grow ripe next to you
until to the ground we fall

Crying boys

Crying boys

telling each other we were joking all this time

playing hard to get
I guess my feelings are hard to guess
but yours
yours are all open
you love me, your feelings have spoken
and yes,
we might have said "I hate you" to each other
ones or twice along the way
but that just happens sometimes
when people love each other too much,
they say
and yes,
we might have gotten on each other's nerves,
but we have worked on each other' s love too
and I might have gotten angry a lot
but I meant it when I said I got you
we said things, a lot of them
but we always cared and that should be a sign
guess this is the part where we should just say
that the mean things were jokes all this time

Crying boys

breaking your heart for the purpose of art

remember how you
used to write sad songs about me?
please let me break your heart,
so you can do that again for me

because I love it when you are
a hopeless romantic for me
doing things you never did for any lover
it's amazing how you love
but it's going to be fascinating when I'm done
and you're going to break even harder

Crying boys

transformation

you are like a caterpillar
no, I'm not telling a cliched story
about the caterpillar turning into a butterfly
you are the caterpillar
that never goes into transformation
you are just fine the way you are
but you're still deserving of the butterfly effect
to make one small act
flourish into a beautiful reality

Crying boys

"I want you and me"

your skin is brown
like honey sprinkled with cacao
I promise I won't get all poetic now
the paleness of your heart
is what I want to point out
personality traits floating around
in the vagueness of summer clouds

in the vagueness of our whereabouts
I guess it's time to get honest now
love in your hands,
hate in your mouth
guess our plans of romance
went all the way south

courage has to be found
to admit our wrongs
to get rid of our fronts
because we have already seen each other naked
so what is it that you are so afraid of?
your mind is so sticky,
maybe honey is what you are made of

Crying boys

boys like me

have I ever mentioned
that I am a sucker for attention
I might be addicted
I might need an intervention
the girl I love the most once said
I must have fallen hard on my head,
wondering whether it's not a silly boys thing
accountability says it's my personality
having trouble to accept my flaws
have I ever mentioned
that I have killed just for attention
and when a boy like me gets caught
we are used to causing nasty dissension

Crying boys

sad communication

I am in a receptive mode
I want to hear what you have to say
finally I am listening
I am open to change my ways
I will face
whatever you have to say
that will hurt me
you are allowed to even yell
until your anger starts to concern me
and your screams break my shell
this is such an awkward situation
we both are afraid to start communicating
this is such a sad conversation

Crying boys

you listen

~~I know~~
~~I said what I said, but actually~~
~~I do think kind of differently now~~
~~please give me space to grow~~
~~like I gave you because I'm just~~
~~as human as you are~~
~~I know I can be a little this or that~~
~~I know I can be distant and sad~~
~~and say I'm alright when I'm not okay~~
~~and say~~ <u>never mind</u> ~~when I have a lot to say~~
~~but you don't have to adjust for me~~
<u>forget it</u> ~~just listen to me,~~
~~like I do to you too~~
~~and you don't have to forget what I did~~
~~but don't forget all the things you did too~~
~~please listen to what you want~~
~~and not what your pride wants to see~~
~~because I don't want you to end up killing me~~

Crying boys

let's pretend

to what extent,
are you willing to pretend?
what or who has to die,
for you to see your lies?

everything that happened
didn't happen to make us happy
it happened to make us learn
and all the art we made
we didn't make it for eyes
but we made it for our minds
and all the mean things we said
we didn't say them to hurt
we said it to make us feel
all the love we gave
we gave to be loved back
not sure we ever cared
if that love was even real

Crying boys

you said forever

shocked but not surprised
it's on me for having loved
a bad guy with angelic eyes
"forever" was the clue
that heaven and hell
were in disguise
but then your hugs became hits
until your words
became the abyss
guess we never know for sure
how long forever really is

Crying boys

lady of justice?

my best coping mechanism
for all the cruelties of this place
was knowing you were just as human,
as I told myself I was in this case
maybe that's why I became
friends with the enemy on that day
you and me were never parallel
we always were the same
now they have given her a name
it's the lady of justice of the night
causing trouble with her scales
deciding and weighing,
who gets to be right

Crying boys

one of us deserves to get hurt

remember that heart I gave you?
I would like it back
and give back all my time too
while you are at it
but you can keep the texts,
And I do want back all the favors
and don't forget your troubles
on the way to the door
because I'm already tangled
in my own anger,
so I don't need your mess
on my floor

Crying boys

the magician

let me show you a magic trick
I overwhelm you with love
until it makes you sick

then I nurse you back
to perfect health,
making you feel things
that you have never felt

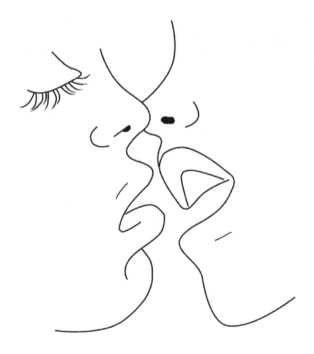

Crying boys

real men cry

I sat down every day
spending some time
to write love letters
that don't even rhyme
and then lied to myself
that they weren't about you
and that all I needed
was someone new
and one day I felt the tears
but real men
aren't suppose to cry
but that was never the truth
now was it?
I was telling myself stupid lies

Crying boys

that it burns means that it's working

all these flowers in the garden
feel so soft
and smell so good
yet both of us are reaching for nettles
that burn so well
and hurt so good

Crying boys

who is going to admit it first?

I can feel you thinking about me
wondering what I'm doing
whenever I cross your mind
I can even feel how you try to forget
all that you love about me,
and we reached a point
where there is nothing left to hate
all there is is this longing state
in which we both crave
each other's voices
who is going to admit it first?
because our desiccated hearts
are dehydrating from thirst

Crying boys

crying girls

the problem was
I made you more important
than you actually were
I gave you more credit
than you actually deserve
I gave you more love
than you could even comprehend
and you made me look
so incredibly stupid in the end

Crying boys

boys who apologize

I go to the train
I mumble your name
hoping some telepathic connection
is to be gained
no pretty girls share your face
I'm dying to hear your voice
is it now too late?
but for you, it's never
and that's a road towards trouble
sorry that I just came out of my bubble
I now hear you a lot
sorry that I didn't when you cried
and when I said I didn't care
I honestly lied
sorry I didn't cry
but see, I do now
I hope you can forgive me some how
I swear I can feel
all kinds of feelings now,
but me breaking your heart was on you
I am not responsible for those wounds

Crying boys

boys

I guess boys aren't as cool
as I always thought them to be
and boys should be
held just as accountable
as we do with little girls

and men aren't as mentally stable
as I always give them credit to be
they aren't as emotionless
as I was always wishing to be

Crying boys

a loving narcissist

you are beautiful
and by beautiful
I mean all that attracts the eyes
and you might also
have an acceptable heart
but that is only
because you love me with it,
and you even might have
a pretty cool mind
but that is only because you
admire my kind with it
you give me all, I suck you dry
then I throw you away
and say my goodbyes,
and you might actually be
a wonderful girl
but that is only as long
as you live in my world

Crying boys

baggage

letting go of pride
feels like a bag
that has been weighing on your shoulder
causing your arm to go numb,
and as soon as you take it off,
the blood in your arm
starts to slowly flow again,
and you might feel sore for a couple days
but feeling the flow will take that away

Crying boys

am I allowed to ever feel?

I forgot how to feel hurt
I forgot how to be bitter
those are feelings I felt
because I claimed
the most feminine parts of me
because my masculine sides
got called ugly,
even though they are the shoulders
my femininity cries on
which is ironic
because every man in someway,
has been got called the cause for tears
but a man and masculinity
are most definitely not the same thing

Crying boys

crying boy meets dying boy

our minds are slithering on each other
like our fingertips used to do
dying boy, more like crying boy
you used to be so cool
how many times did you have to hear
"I told you so"
for you to see you're such a fool?
I'm not bitter about it,
it's actually pretty sweet
kind of sour when you mentioned,
that without me, you're incomplete
but that's on me, boy
you're not dying, you're just crying
don't you see, boy?
I got a little cocky, so to say
that is nothing compared to your upheaval of pride
I might have became the most evil guy

Crying boys

it's nice to be the prize

roads and roads
wanting to go home
I'm sorry, it's getting boring,
without you blowing up my phone
thoughts and thoughts
we should talk about them more
teens becoming adults
never know how they feel for sure
patience and compassion
how could we ever overlook it?
to be honest, I have no heart,
so when I noticed yours I just took it

Crying boys

text received

I hate all love songs
I hate all pick-up lines
I hate that there are billions of people,
but it bothers me that you aren't mine
and I hate crying
and even feeling anything
I hate birthdays and holidays,
and the only way for me to love again
is if you just let me see your face
because you remind me of everything
I simply don't want to hate

Crying boys

disgusted by love

I have had enough of being my own muse
just because you make me feel misunderstood
I don't want to feel like we've built a wall
just to fall in love again after all
now, you're begging me for reconciliation
don't you worry,
your love is my destination
you can help me navigate through all your tears
I would love to hear your sobbing in my ears
your kisses feel like such a long time ago
it feels like our lips never drove down this road,
but it doesn't matter what I do or what I say,
we both will make each other feel okay

Crying boys

I want to say that I'm missing her

closer
the closer we get
and the closer the electronics
the stronger the connection,
and I'm not wondering
if you are anywhere near me
because I know you are and I am sure
that tomorrow here with me you will be
closer
to my connection
so strong
through electronics, I feel your affection
I hear your craving, I hear your breath
I even hear you thinking that this distance is bad
intentions, you want my attention?
firstly, there is an apology you forgot to mention
I haven't forgot, cause you have hurt me a lot
I should be strong enough to not want one
but maybe I am not
but what does it matter?
we are connected
we went from bad reception
to new inceptions

Crying boys

parallel universes

they say opposites attract
but universes don't,
you thought that you would fade
but your heart knew that you wouldn't
staring in the glaze of your own eyes
begging to see my face
you don't want this universe
if it's the opposite of my way
but universes overlap
that is the only way we
touch again
that's the way we
always met
that is how we
currently love again
so I choose this journey
for us
to make our minds
overlap
and become one
universe
in this ordinary time

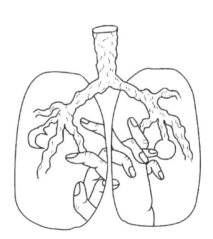

Crying boys

it's quiet until we scream

it's quiet
but only as quiet as it gets in your head
your sorrows are being loud
I hear worries about the things you've said
please let it get to your head
I want to see your tears, like the ones I have shed
but don't worry
I promise I'm not mad
we have it good,
and the worse has already passed
I don't even want a sorry anymore
sorry or not, I know you feel regret
but it might have to be said
scream and cry out your sorrows
please go ahead
I want to see your eyes go red

Crying boys

I am important

it's cold without my fire
it's warm without the chills that I create
and without me as your light
your nights are spent wide awake
you care more than I do,
and all I care about is me
but don't you worry
you fit perfectly
in the plans I have for me
my mind fits with yours
like two people holding hands
all I now know is how to make me glow
and on me, your happiness now depends
our hands were never friends,
but our bodies always kissed
and that is less romantic than it sounds
or perhaps, less than you would've wished

Crying boys

one last time

one lie
I swear this is the last one
one lie that I feel fine
that I am okay
with my past mistakes
one lie
the last untruthful thing I say
one last sweat, one last pat on the back
one last,
"oh, there is nothing wrong with that"
my last poor decision
I'm sober from my addiction
yeah yeah, I said this before
bad, bad decisions
I look more beautiful this way
I will keep this new face
this "I will change" will not go to waste
give me one last lie that I'm allowed to taste

Crying boys

unfortunate trauma's

bandaids and bandages
enemies and savages
who is to blame? who deserves the flames?
but to a big realization, I then came
attacks from the outside causes turmoil inside
I can stitch up the wounds,
but they are things I can't hide
I can shed tears,
and let nightmares keep me up at night
but this is not a matter
of out of sight out of mind
it is out of sight, but very much alive
wearing cozy feelings,
while the pain still thrives

maybe that is just a reminder
that I am very much alive

deprived of the pain
cleaning the remains and stains
loving who I am
regardless of the flaws I contain
accepting what has happened
and seeing I became more wonderful
than I could've ever imagined

Crying boys

let's enhance the romance

I should tell you
about all the poetry
I have written from a broken heart
I should tell you
about all the letters
I have written out of love,
and it is never in a romantic way,
which somehow makes it more exciting
but we know what we should feel
because we have already decided it
in our heads
and this is the script we live by
because there is no
meant to be
we create things
to be

Crying boys

where have you been?

I am so ready to hear
about your journey
all the the things you learned
all the misery you felt
all the gratitude you now feel
all the truth you denied
but now gratefully see
I want to hear about
how you are still the same person
but with a much better self

Crying boys

Woman and their femininity

I have a hard time dealing with
the prodigiousness in you
because you are intimidating in such a graceful way
I see you as the foundation of a temple
and your body is the sight I have
been blessed enough to admire
in how it carries your personality
your body carries more than just your own experiences
of life and all its phraseologies
but you I admire, not for what you complete or create
but for the creation you are on your own

Outside of femininity

and if I'm right, you don't need me telling you
about how you have been created from particles
our humanity has no comprehension of,
and I hope never to find out how we created
the mind we call the opposite of feminine
because I don't believe life to be black and white
this is why I have dedicated an entire collection to your ways
because it fascinates me
in how it complicates our psyche
but simply completes our entire universe

Crying boys

A note to a friend

Dear friend,

I wrote a letter to you to tell you how much I changed. But then, something happened just when I wanted to share what I overcame. So let me share now before I change my mind.

I was expressing how euphoric it made me feel to be who I am. The reason I wrote all these poems. I feel like an addict, and this feels like a relapse. I felt like my heart broke all over again. I thought it would never happen again. I didn't cry this time, but I felt something again after numbing myself for such a long time. Maybe, I was just addicted and attached to who I was. But I'm letting go right now. The title of this collection was supposed to be a metaphor for how scared boys can be to show emotions. But I guess it was close to who I still was. I wrote poems about who I am while I thought I was writing poems about who I was. Growing is not something you choose to do when things go wrong. It's a consistent lifestyle that has to be maintained. I was suppose to hold on to who I became because she truly might be the best version of me. But I then learned, that who I am and who I want to be is the same person.
The good news is I remembered that as soon as I relapsed. I am moving forward. This time will be faster because I know what I have to do. I try never to be hard on myself and tell myself that I am allowed to feel. Because experiencing emotions is the

Crying boys

most human we will ever be. Now I also know that there is more to life than just the plans we make for it.

Thank you for listening to me. I appreciate it with everything in me. You always find a way to teach me things. The past is the present as long as we feel the same now as we did then. Feeling the same feelings, is living the same life. But if we learn to feel differently, specifically in a better manner, the past will not repeat itself. You taught me that without knowing it, and I'm grateful for that lesson either way.

Sincerely,

friend

Crying boys

Thank you.

Made in the USA
Columbia, SC
06 June 2020